PEGASUS ENCYCLOPEDIA LIBRARY

Transport
LAND TRANSPORT

Edited by: Pallabi B. Tomar
Managing editor: Tapasi De
Designed by: Vijesh Chahal, Anil Kumar and Rohit Kumar
Illustrated by: Suman S. Roy, Tanoy Choudhury
Colouring done by: Vinay Kumar, Sonu, Kiran Kumari & Pradeep Kumar

LAND TRANSPORT

CONTENTS

What is land transport? 3

History of land transport 4

Categories of land transportation 7

Types of land transport vehicles 8

Roads and highways 12

Traffic control 14

Advantages of road transport 16

Disadvantages 17

Land transport and environment 18

Some famous land transportation vehicles 21

Test Your Memory 31

Index 32

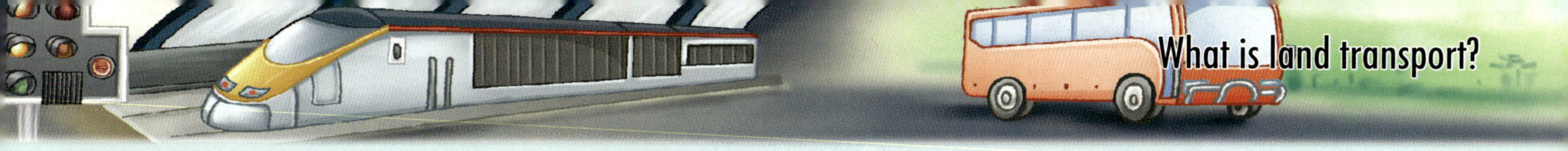

What is land transport?

Land transport includes vehicles which neither sail on the oceans nor fly in the air. This means land transport consists of cars, vans, buses, two-wheelers, trains and a couple of other vehicles which travel on the roads. Bicycles also fall into this transport category.

But land transport did not impact the environment and climate until the invention of the engine driven vehicles. When people began to make use of fossil fuels in order to run these vehicles, and in the process increased pollution, scientists began to find ways to make land transport more environment friendly. The amount of these vehicles has been virtually exploding in the last century and is still growing, particularly in the developing countries.

This is the main form of transportation in the world today. People move about land with the help of their own power, use domestic animals or use a combination of the wheel with electric or fuel powered engines to move people and freight quickly and efficiently.

Astonishing fact

An average new car today consumes 15 per cent less fuel per 100 km than 10 years ago.

LAND TRANSPORT

History of land transport

Land transportation first began with the carrying of goods by people. The ancient civilizations of Central America, Mexico and Peru transported materials in that fashion over long roads and bridges.

The first road vehicles were two-wheeled carts, with crude disks fashioned from stone serving as the wheels. Used by the Sumerians (c.3000 B.C.), such simple wagons were precursors of the chariot, which the Egyptians and Greeks, among others, developed from a lumbering cart into a work of beauty. Under the Chou dynasty (c.1000 B.C.), the Chinese constructed the world's first permanent road system. The Romans built 85,000 km of roads, primarily for military reasons, throughout their vast empire. The most famous of these was the Appian Way which begun in 325 B.C.

Four-wheeled carriages were developed towards the end of the 12th century; they transported only the privileged until the late 18th century, when Paris licensed **omnibuses** and **stagecoaches** began to operate in England. In the United States the demands of an ever-extending frontier led to the creation of the **Conestoga wagon** and the **prairie schooner**, so that goods and families could be transported across the eastern mountains, the Great Plains, and westward.

The great period of railroad building in the second half of the 19th century made earlier methods of transportation largely obsolete within the United States. After World War I, however, automobiles, buses, and trucks came to exceed the railroads in importance.

> The first bus, known as a carrosse, was introduced in Paris by Blaise Pascal, in 1662. It was horse-drawn and carried eight people. Carosses was a great innovation, as it ran every few minutes.

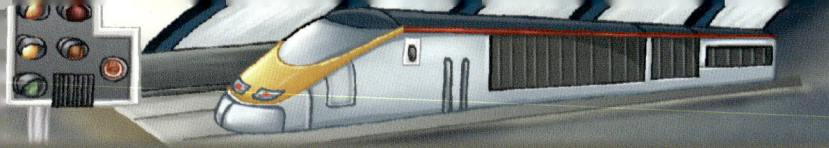

History of land transport

Compared to transport by boats and ships, transportation on land was slower, more uncomfortable and more dangerous. Goods were transported on rivers and on the seas, rather than over land. Nevertheless, the Roman Empire had an excellent system of roads. The army built most of the roads because they allowed soldiers to travel quickly in wartime and formed a basis for the administration of the Empire. Some of the old roads are still used today. However, the roads made it also easier for the merchants to transport goods around the Roman Empire.

The actual means of transportation were provided by horses, donkeys, animal-pulled vehicles and of course by foot. Horses had problems with the metalled road surfaces and wore hippo sandals to protect their feet. These objects have been found in small numbers.

The earliest forms of road transport were horses or oxen, which carried goods over dirt tracks. Military officers travelled on the back of a horse and the army had stations at which an officer or courier could exchange a tired horse for a fresh one.

Most of the time, the traders also went on foot or used a donkey or horse to ride on it. They put the goods into bags, which hung at the sides of the donkey, because they couldn't afford wooden carts. For the transport of heavier and bigger amounts of goods the Romans used wagons, made out of wood, pulled by horses or oxen. As the roads were paved with hard-wearing stone slabs, transport was not very comfortable either for the animal or for the merchant.

Coventry Machine Company made the first all-metal bicycle called Ariel in 1870. It was the first machine to have wheels with wire spokes.

LAND TRANSPORT

The wagons, which were used for transporting goods, had either 2 or 4 wheels. These wheels may have been simple wooden disks or had 8, sometimes even up to 12 spokes. They were banded with iron. The heavier carts, made out of oak wood, were pulled by oxen and the lighter ones by horses or mules. The plaustrum was one of the earliest and simplest four-wheel vehicles found in Rome. It was just a flat board on wheels.

When a number of people needed to travel together or when goods or luggage had to be carried, a four-wheeled wagon called raeda was used. As the Romans did not have harness (the combination of straps, bands, etc. by which a horse is fastened to its loads) suitable for horses, usually heavy wagons were pulled by oxen or mules. The lightest vehicles in general use were two-wheeled carts with a pair of seats perched high up.

The Romans used also various other kinds of vehicles and modes of transport, for instance the lectica, a framework of canvas stretched between two parallel bars, which was similar to an 18th century sedan chair, an enclosed vehicle for one person. This 'portable couch' was used only for rich people and it was carried by slaves.

> **Etienne Lenoir, a Belgian enameller turned engineer who lived in Paris, invented the first motor car in 1862.**

Lectica

Plaustrum

Eduard Delamare-Deboutteville, of Fontaine-le-Bourg, France, made the first petrol-engined car in 1883.

Categories of land transportation

Transport on roads can be roughly grouped into two categories—transportation of goods and transportation of people. In many countries licensing requirements and safety regulations ensure a separation of the two industries.

The nature of road transportation of goods depends, apart from the degree of development of the local infrastructure, on the distance the goods are transported by road, the weight and volume of the individual shipment and the type of goods transported. For short distances and light, small shipments a van or pickup truck maybe used. For large shipments even if less than a full truckload a truck is more appropriate. In some countries cargo is transported by road in horse-drawn carriages, donkey carts or other non-motorized mode. Delivery services are sometimes considered a separate category from cargo transport. In many places fast food is transported on roads by various types of vehicles. People are transported on roads either in individual cars or automobiles or public transports like bus, trains, etc. Special modes of individual transport by road like rickshaws or velotaxis may also be locally available.

LAND TRANSPORT

Types of land transport vehicles

Ground transport was present during prehistoric times first from simple sledges that were made from multiple pieces of tree branches tied together to later the creation of two-wheeled carts made from stone that were shaped to a disc to form the wheels. It wasn't until the 12th century that the first four-wheeled horse drawn carriage was created to transport the rich and the privileged.

It was much later during the 18th century where omnibuses and stagecoaches were employed in England, Paris and other various parts of Europe. The United States soon followed pursuit utilizing what was known as the **prairie schooner** and **Conestoga wagon**. These not only allowed them to transport goods and people over flat land but also through rough terrains and mountain areas. With the continuous growth in need for transportation of goods and people, the railway system soon took over in the United States, providing connections to most major cities and isolated country sites and farms. However, it was until after World War I, that car, buses, trucks came into use and exceeded the importance of railroads services.

> Karl Benz of Mannheim, Germany, made the first successful petrol-engined car in 1885. It was driven for the first time in 1886 at a little over nine miles an hour.

Today, the world's ground transportation is like a web that can take you or any goods to any destination at any time. Each country has its own transport infrastructure and network that delivers the needs to its population. The basic land transport network usually includes the following:

1. **Automobiles**
   - Car
   - Taxi
   - Bus
2. **Railway System**
   - Train
   - Tram
3. **Other Ground Transportation**
   - Motorcycle
   - Bicycle

Car

Cars are also commonly known as motor cars and automobiles. They are wheeled vehicles.

It is either powered by fuel such as petrol, diesel, LPG, etc. The act of operating the vehicle is called driving. In a vehicle, there is a seat for the driver and two or more passenger seats.

Taxi

Taxi is a form of public transport on the ground where a driver picks up a passenger or several passengers who wish to travel to the same destination upon request.

Fee is charge as per kilometre or location. Although, taxi is a form of public transport, but at any one given time the driver will be only taking one or a group of passengers who will be going to the same destination.

Bus

The word 'bus' arises from the Latin word omnibus meaning 'for all'. Omnibuses were first used in 1662 in Paris, France and at that time they were drawn by horses.

In the early 20th century motorized buses powered by gasoline or diesel came into use, and it was able to take passengers to places where trains could not reach. Today, buses are one of the most common forms of public transport used in most major cities around the world. It is used to take commuters to work, home and shopping. It is used as a school bus, tour bus, etc.

Gottlieb Daimler of Cannstatt, Germany, produced the first four-wheeled car at the same time as Karl Benz, also driven in 1886. Since then, both firms continued to develop various cars until the consolidation of Daimler-Benz in 1926.

LAND TRANSPORT

Gottlieb Daimler built the first motor cycle in 1885. It was ridden by his son, Paul, for six miles.

Train

Another commonly used land transport around the world is trains. It can consist of a single or multiple connected rail vehicles which are interconnected and move together along a railway system. Trains can transport passengers travelling between stations where distance can vary from under 1 km to much more. It is also used as freight trains to carry goods in bulk over long distances. Transporting goods via freight trains is highly economical and energy efficient when transporting long distances.

There are many other special kinds of trains that run on special 'railways'. They are **atmospheric railways**, **monorails** (single rail trains), high-speed railways (**bullet trains** seen in Japan), maglev, **rubber-tired underground, funicular** and **cog railways**.

Tram

The tram is also known as the tramcar, trolley and streetcar which travels wholly or partly along a form of railway system or tracks laid on city streets. They are designed to transport passengers within close range villages, towns and cities. It is only on rare occasion that they are used as freight to transport goods.

Almost all passenger trams are propelled by an electric motor which is fed from an overhead line especially designed to run on tracks set up on public roads. Due to road developments and the increased use of private vehicles on roads, the use of trams as a form of transport has decreased dramatically.

Motorcycle

A motorcycle is a two-wheeled motor vehicle resembling a heavy bicycle, sometimes having two saddles and a sidecar with a third wheel. There are many different types of motorcycles. These can include standard bikes, road motorcycles, cruiser, sport bikes, touring and sport bikes, scooters, mopeds and much more. The first motor tricycle was built in 1884 in England, and the first gasoline-engine motorcycle was built by Gottlieb Daimler in 1885. Motorcycles were widely used after 1910, especially by the armed forces in World War I. After 1950 a larger, heavier motorcycle was used mainly for touring and sport competitions. The moped, a light, low-speed motor bicycle that can also be pedalled, was developed mainly in Europe, and the sturdier Italian-made motor scooter also became popular for its economy.

Bicycle

Bicycles are also commonly called a bike. It is a light-framed two-wheeled vehicle that is driven by the movement of constant pedalling of a pedal by a person. All bicycles are fitted with pneumatic tyres, with the rear wheel being propelled by the rider through a crank, chain and gear mechanism.

Bicycles are becoming more and more popular because it is environmentally friendly as it does not turn out any toxic gases in to the air. It is also a great way to exercise.

Hildebrand Wolfmuller, of Munich, Germany, manufactured the first motor cycle for sale to the public in 1894, the same year that Aleandre Darracq of France, began to manufacture them too.

LAND TRANSPORT

Roads and highways

In many countries, roads and highways provide the dominant mode of land transportation. They form the backbone of the economy, often carrying more than 80 per cent of passengers and over 50 per cent of freight in a country, and providing essential links to vast rural road networks.

Highways are the most important part of the automobile industry. If there were no roads or highways there would be no need for automobiles. Highways allow drivers to get from destination to destination within cities and states. Highways can be large or small in the number of lanes available in each direction. There are different highway designs across the world. Highways can consist of tunnels, bridges and even ferries.

Of the various modes of transport that connect the cities and villages of the country, road transport constitutes the crucial link. Road infrastructure facilitates movement of men and material, helps trade and commerce, links industry and agriculture to markets and opens up backward regions. In addition, the road system also provides last-mile (final leg of the journey) connection for other modes of transport such as railways, airports, ports and inland waterway transport and complements the efforts of these modes in meeting the needs of transportation.

Trams reduce congestion in city centres by providing people with a quick, reliable, high-quality alternative to the car. They can reduce road traffic by up to 14 per cent.

Roads and highways

Roads are the vital lifelines of the economy making possible trade and commerce. Roads are the most preferred modes of transportation and considered as one of the cost effective modes of transportation. Roads are easily accessible to each individual. Roads facilitate movement of both men and materials anywhere within a country. It helps in socio-economic development as well as brings national integration. An efficient and well-established network of roads is desired for promoting trade and commerce in any country and also fulfils the needs of a sound transportation system for sustained economic development.

Roads are among the most important public assets in many countries. Improvements of roads bring immediate and sometimes dramatic benefits to communities through better access to hospitals, schools and markets; greater comfort, speed, and safety; and lower vehicle operating costs.

For these benefits to be sustained, however, road improvements must be followed by well-planned programs of road maintenance. Without regular maintenance, roads can rapidly fall into disrepair, preventing communities from reaping the longer term benefits of road improvement such as increased agricultural production and an increase in school enrolment.

Although the need for maintenance is widely recognized, it is still not adequately implemented in many countries. Many countries spend just 20–50 per cent of what they should be spending on maintenance of their road network.

LAND TRANSPORT

Traffic control

Nearly all roadways are built with devices meant to control traffic. Most notable to the motorist are those meant to communicate directly with the driver. Broadly, these fall into three categories—signs, signals or pavement markings. They help the driver navigate, assign the right-of-way at intersections, indicate laws such as speed limits and parking regulations, advise of potential hazards, indicate passing and no passing zones and assures traffic is orderly and safe.

200 years ago these devices were signs, nearly all informal. In the late 19th century signals began to appear in the biggest cities at a few highly congested intersections. They were manually operated, and consisted of semaphores, flags or paddles, or in some cases coloured electric lights, all modelled on railroad signals. In the 20th century signals were automated, at first with electromechanical devices and later with computers. Signals can be quite sophisticated with vehicle sensors embedded in the pavement, the signal can control and choreograph the turning movements of heavy traffic in the most complex of intersections. In the 1920s traffic engineers learned how to coordinate signals along a thoroughfare to increase its speeds and volumes. In the 1980s, with computers, similar coordination of whole networks became possible.

Traffic is the business of moving people and cargo from one place to another. Farmers have to transfer their products from their farms to the market and this involves a lot of movement. Goods are also in need of transporting from the manufacturing plants to the stores, etc. There's a need to manage the movement of individuals and goods in a safe and efficient manner. We must understand that effective transportation of goods from place to place gets rid of cost and, consequently, keeps the costs of goods down. Good traffic control management likewise helps lower the probability of accidents occurring.

Traffic control

All means of transportation require productive traffic control. In air traffic control, the management has to be very effective in order to avoid the collision of airplanes that are taking off and making landings. Clearance has to be provided by the air traffic controller alone as they monitor the number of airplanes that are supposed to arrive at a particular scheduled time. Doing this, the traffic controllers can guide the airplane traffic safely and efficiently.

In road traffic, traffic lights can be very helpful to manage traffic at intersections. The colours of these traffic lights guide the drivers on when to stop or when to go thereby preventing cars from colliding. A separate lane for automobiles turning left or right can be provided with a lighted arrow to minimize interference with opposing traffic. A separate lane can be provided with a lighted green arrow permitting the autos to turn left without opposing traffic.

The most common road accidents occur when drivers do not obey the traffic lights. Drivers endanger themselves and other people whenever they don't follow the traffic lights. Statistics show that reckless driving causes more accidents and injuries to individuals and pedestrians than when drivers drive defensively and safely.

Traffic control also involves traffic rules and laws to be followed. Strict execution of these laws and rules will efficiently regulate the smooth and orderly flow of traffic on the road. Traffic control is the organization of numerous rules, traffic signals or signs, marked lanes, intersections and junctions. Some may have thorough or complex road rules while others will rely more on the driver's good sense in safe driving.

Good traffic control management is also essential in construction zones, road repairs, functions and events, and road disruptions caused by accidents. Efficient control is very important as a way to effectively handle the flow of automobiles and pedestrians in these situations.

15

LAND TRANSPORT

Advantages of road transport

Road transport has the following advantages:-

- It is a relatively cheaper mode of transport as compared to the other modes.

- Perishable goods can be transported at a faster speed by road carriers over a short distance.

- It is a flexible mode of transport as loading and unloading is possible at any destination. It provides door-to-door service.

- It helps people to travel and carry goods from one place to another, in places which are not connected by other means of transport like hilly areas.

- It is reliable as goods are under direct control of the drivers.

- It is relatively safe for goods since there is little handling.

Disadvantages

It has the following limitations:-

- Due to limited carrying capacity, road transport is not economical for long distance transportation of goods.
- Transportation of heavy goods or goods in bulk by road involves high cost.
- It is affected by adverse weather conditions. Floods, rain, landslide, etc., sometimes create obstructions to land transport.
- It is a slower mode of transportation.
- Land transport burns more of our already diminishing fossil fuels.
- There is also a higher risk of accident.

Land transport and environment

The issue of land transport and the environment is paradoxical in nature. From one side, land transport increases the mobility demands of passengers and freight. This takes into consideration both local and international trade. On the other side, transport activities have resulted in growing levels of motorization and congestion. As a result, the land transport sector is becoming increasingly linked to environmental problems. With a technology relying heavily on the combustion of hydrocarbons, notably with the internal combustion engine, the impacts of land transport over environmental systems has increased with motorization. This has reached a point where transportation activities are a dominant factor behind the emission of most pollutants and thus affecting the environment.

The impact of land transport on the environment is a subject of growing concern. Roads and traffic are variously condemned for increasing the noise levels, poor childhood respiratory health, loss of wildlife habitat, the division and dislocation of communities and many other manifestations of social and environmental pathology.

Land transport also affects water quality because oil and particles from vehicles get washed into creeks and rivers. In urban environments, run-off from roads goes into storm water drains. These feed into creeks and rivers, which eventually meet the sea.

Land transport and environment

Oil is a particularly harmful water pollutant. Even a small amount of oil can severely contaminate waterways. Oil can be toxic to aquatic life and smother plants and animals.

Particles from the wear of tyres, brakes and other components get washed into the storm water and pollute waterways.

When it rains, air pollution from cars mixes with rainwater and falls to the ground, adding to water pollution.

Detergents also contaminate waterways.

Cars produce greenhouse gases that contribute to global warming and climate change. The main greenhouse gas is carbon dioxide. Others include nitrous oxide and methane.

Greenhouse gases occur naturally in the atmosphere, trapping some of the heat radiated from the Earth's surface. Increases in the amount of these gases, mainly through the burning of carbon-based fuels such as coal and oil, are increasing the average temperature of the Earth, affecting local climates including temperature and rainfall.

Air pollution has negative health effects, especially for vulnerable people, including those with allergic and respiratory conditions, such as asthma, hay fever and sinusitis, and respiratory and lung conditions commonly associated with the elderly. Research suggests that certain air pollutants (e.g. benzene) are carcinogenic.

LAND TRANSPORT

Vehicle exhaust emissions are a major source of air pollution in some areas, particularly around busy road corridors. Pollutants include carbon monoxide (CO), nitrogen dioxide (NO2), benzene and particulate matter.

Heavy metals and petroleum products from vehicles can contaminate both land and water. Land transport is also responsible for some of the extensive heavy metal contamination of some harbours and estuarine areas. Contaminated water can make water unsafe to swim in or drink. Culverts for transport infrastructure can disrupt fish migration. Suspended sediments from road works for example, can affect water clarity, favouring species that prefer cloudy conditions.

Noise and vibrations can affect people who live or work near busy roads or rail facilities. This can cause stress, exacerbate existing medical conditions and interfere with daily activities such as communicating or sleeping. High levels of noise can also bring down property values.

Some famous land transportation vehicles

Some famous land transportation vehicles

Bugatti Veyron

The Bugatti Veyron 16.4 is the most powerful, most expensive and fastest street-legal production car in the world, with a proven top speed of over 407 km/h. The car is built by Volkswagen AG subsidiary Bugatti Automobiles SAS and is sold under the legendary Bugatti marque. It is named after racing driver Pierre Veyron, who won the 24 hours of Le Mans in 1939 while racing for the original Bugatti firm. The Veyron features a W16 engine—16 cylinders in 4 banks of 4 cylinders.

According to Volkswagen, the final production Veyron engine produces between 1020 and 1040 metric hp (1006 to 1026 SAE net hp), so it makes the Veyron the most powerful production road-car engine in history.

The $1.3 million Veyron will reach a top speed of 407 km/h; a speed it can maintain for 12 minutes before all the fuel is gone. The car can hit 96 km/h in just 2.5 seconds, 160 km/h in 5.5 seconds, and 241 km/h in 9.8 seconds. Getting to 322 km/h takes 18.3 seconds and 402 km/h takes 42.3 seconds.

A special key is required to unlock the Veyron's top speed of 407 km/h. The car is then lowered to just 3.5 inches from the ground. A hydraulic spoiler extends at speed, and it can also serve as an air brake.

21

LAND TRANSPORT

Rolls-Royce Phantom

The Rolls-Royce Phantom is a luxury saloon automobile made by Rolls-Royce Motor Cars, a BMW subsidiary. It was launched in 2003 and is the first Rolls-Royce model made under the ownership of BMW. It has a 6.8 L, 48-valve, V12 engine that produces 453 hp (338 kW) and 531 ft·lbf (720 N·m) of torque. The engine is derived from BMW's existing V12 power plant. It is 1.63 m (63 in) tall, 1.99 m (74.8 in) wide, 5.83 m (228 in) long, and weighs 2485 kg (5478 lb). The body of the car is built on an aluminium space frame and the Phantom can accelerate to 100 km/h (60 mph) in 5.7 seconds.

The Rolls Royce Phantom is a premium ultra luxury sedan offered in extended and regular wheelbase model that provides comfortable seating capacity for five passengers. Most expected standard features include cast aluminium 21 inch wheels, Lexicon Logic 7 15-speaker surround sound system with satellite radio with lifetime subscription, single-CD in dash player, auxiliary audio jack and glove box mounted six-CD changer, adjustable air suspension, multifunction electronics controller, rear and front parking sensors, Rolls-Royce Assist emergency telematics, power-closing rear coach doors, voice command functionality, power closing trunk lid, power front soft close doors, navigation system, sunroof, keyless ignition, multizone climate control, Bluetooth, heated rear and front seats, veneered picnic tables built in rear seatbacks, driver memory functions, leather headliner with cashmere and wool accent panels and power telescoping and tilt steering column.

Some famous land transportation vehicles

Tata Trucks

Tata trucks are amongst the most sought-after heavy commercial vehicles (HCV) in India. Tata Motors is the fourth largest truck manufacturer in the world. Established in 1945, it first rolled out its vehicle in 1954. Since then, more than 4 million Tata vehicles run on Indian roads. It has its manufacturing units located in various locations across the country including Jamshedpur, Pantnagar, Pune, Dharwad and Lucknow.

Tata trucks have created a niche in the truck industry worldwide. Tata trucks also lead in the key medium and heavy truck category with an index of 90 in the segment of Tractor-Trailer.

Volvo Trucks

Volvo is the second largest producer of heavy duty trucks in the world. There are few countries you can visit where there isn't a Volvo truck on the road.

Based in Sweden, Volvo trucks is a truck manufacturer owned by the Volvo Group. The company currently employs over 22,000 people around the world and has its global headquarters in Gothenburg.

Volvo trucks produce and sell over 100,000 trucks each year. Approximately 95 per cent of the trucks they produce are in the heavy weight class above 16 tons. A large proportion of Volvo trucks are manufactured in the USA along with Sweden, Brazil and Belgium.

Volvo trucks are renowned for their safety record and are considered to be some of the safest vehicles in the world. They are also incredibly reliable and durable.

LAND TRANSPORT

Trans-Siberian Express

The Trans Siberian Express travels 9,297 km between Moscow and Vladivostok. The line opened in 1914 and is the world's longest continuous rail line.

The **Trans-Siberian Railway** or Transsib is the name given to the three rail routes that traverse Siberia from Moscow.

- The **Trans-Mongolian** goes from Moscow to Beijing, China via Ulaanbaatar, Mongolia.
- The **Trans-Manchurian** travels through Siberia and Chinese Manchuria to Beijing.
- The **Trans-Siberian** proper goes from Moscow to the Pacific terminus of Vladivostok.

The Trans-Siberian Railway is the longest railway in the world. It was built between 1891 and 1916 to connect Moscow with the Far-East city of Vladivostok. En route it passes through the cities of Perm, Yekaterinburg, Omsk, Novosibirsk, Krasnoyarsk, Irkutsk, Chita and Khabarovsk.

Some famous land transportation vehicles

Eurostar

The Eurostar service was launched on November 14, 1994, to carry passengers between London, Paris and Brussels through the channel tunnel. It can reach speeds of 300 km/h. In its first ten years it carried a total of 59 million passengers.

Eurostar is a train service that connects London with Paris and Brussels. Trains cross the English Channel through the Channel Tunnel. In addition to the three destination cities, some Eurostar services currently stop en route at Ashford in Kent and Lille in northern France. Eurostar, which began services in November 1994, is a joint venture between Belgian, French and British railway companies.

The Eurostar service has established a dominant share of the market for travellers on the routes it serves – 68 per cent for London-Paris and 63 per cent for London-Brussels as of November 2004.

25

LAND TRANSPORT

Shinkansen (Bullet trains)

Due to its dense population, Japan dumped its focus on cars and concentrated on shinkansen (Bullet trains), the world fastest scheduled rail services. They were introduced in 1964 to coincide with the Tokyo Olympic Games.

Japan's main islands of Honshu and Kyushu are served by a network of high speed train lines that connect Tokyo with most of the country's major cities. Japan's high speed trains (Bullet trains) are called shinkansen and are operated by Japan Railways (JR).

Running at speeds of up to 300 km/h, the shinkansen is known for punctuality (most trains depart on time to the second), comfort (relatively silent cars with spacious, always forward facing seats), safety (no fatal accidents in its history) and efficiency. Thanks to the Japan Rail Pass, the shinkansen can also be a very cost effective means of travel.

The shinkansen network consists of multiple lines, among which the Tokaido Shinkansen (Tokyo - Nagoya - Kyoto - Osaka) is the oldest and the most popular. All shinkansen lines (except the Akita and Yamagata Shinkansen) run on tracks that are exclusively built for and used by shinkansen trains. Most lines are served by multiple train categories, ranging from the fastest category that stops only at major stations to the slowest category that stops at every station along the way.

Some famous land transportation vehicles

Blue Train

This is one of the world's most luxurious trains and it has operated between Cape Town and Tshwane (Pretoria), South Africa since 1939. The train, carriages and decor are mainly blue – hence the name.

It's the most famous train in South Africa, and one of the most famous trains in the world. South Africa's 'Blue Train' links Cape Town with Pretoria once or twice a week, year round. With a one-way fare of about £890 or $1,300 per person for two people travelling together even in the low season, it's now aimed squarely at foreign visitors. Single passengers cannot opt to share, so should reckon on paying £1,330 or $2,030 one-way for sole use of a 2-berth compartment. However, The Blue Train is definitely the most luxurious way to travel between these two cities.

The Blue Train offers two types of room— 'Deluxe' compartments have either a double bed or two single beds and en suite shower or small bath. 'Luxury' compartments cost a bit more and are almost identical, but have a full size bath and a video. The train has a dining car and two lounge cars (one smoking, one non-smoking) and one of the two train sets has an observation car at the rear, allowing you to look back along the line.

LAND TRANSPORT

Harley-Davidson Motorcycle

Known as the motorcycle of motorcycles, Harley Davidson Motorcycles remains constant throughout the ages with its varying style and fashions. Harley-Davidson began in 1901 with William

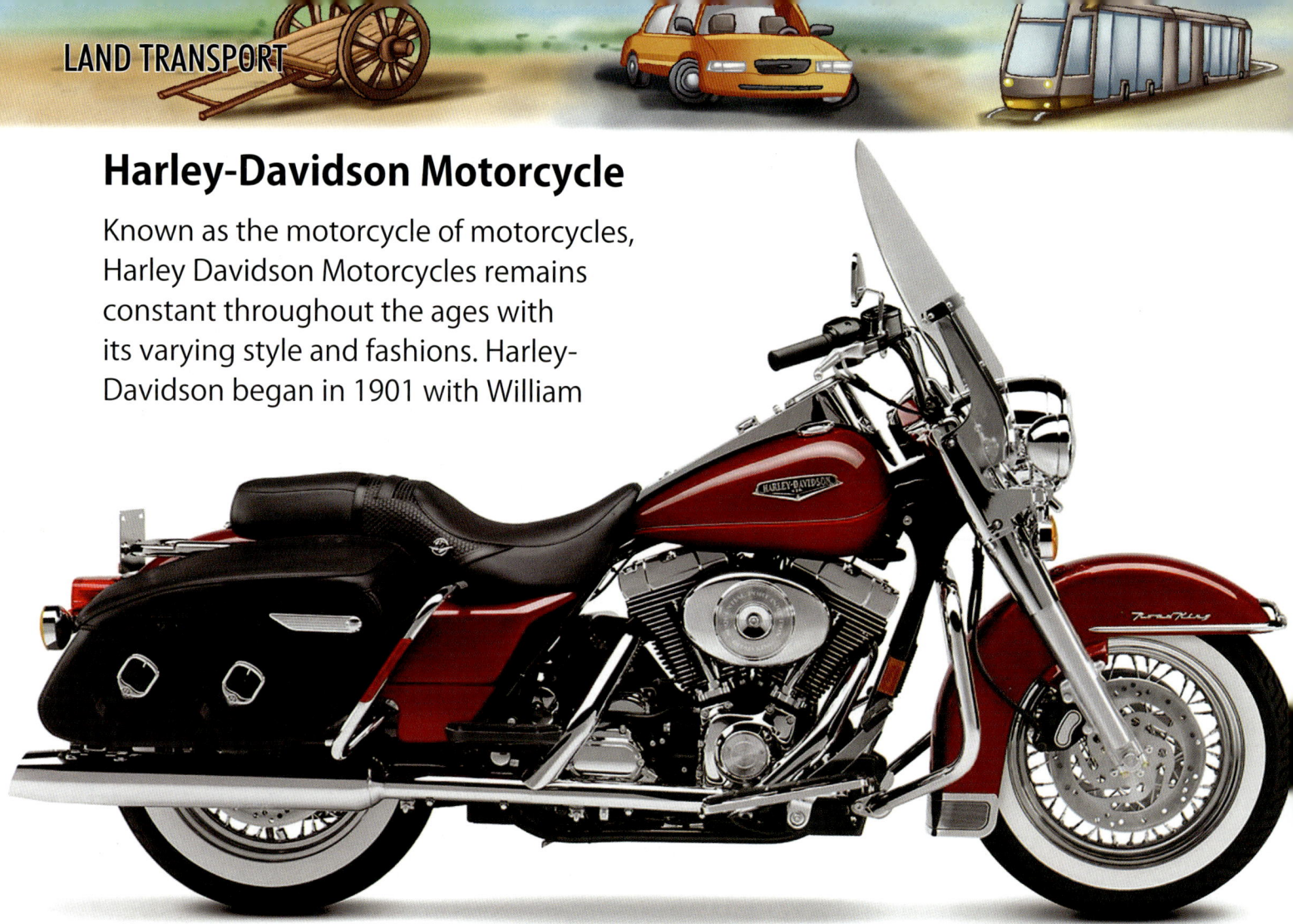

S. Harley and childhood friend Arthur Davidson starting work on a motor-bicycle, with the first motorcycles available to purchase in 1905. The growth of the company included supplying around 15,000 machines to the military forces during World War I, and by 1920, Harley-Davidson was the largest motorcycle manufacturer in the world. In 1929, the flathead engine was introduced, followed by the Knucklehead in 1941. By the outbreak of World War II, only two American motorcycle companies existed, with Harley-Davidson producing over 90,000 military vehicles, and after the war ended, many of these then came back into civilian hands at relatively low prices.

The company produces traditional cruiser motorcycles with V-Twin engines. Popular models of Harley Davidson include the Sportster, Road King, Electra Glide, Dyna Glide and Softail.

The Harley Bikes are ideal for fast rides on the highway. The unique design and the configuration symbolize adventure and wilderness. The engine power starts from 750 cc. This chopper bike is usually meant for sports biking.

Some famous land transportation vehicles

Suzuki Hayabusa

Suzuki Hayabusa is among the most popular sports motorcycles ever produced. Since its inception it is widely regarded as the fastest bike in production in the world. The bike is also known as GSX1300R in some countries. In the unrestricted environment of a racetrack, Hayabusa can thrill anyone with its awesome power.

The Hayabusa's 4-stroke, four-cylinder liquid-cooled 1299cc engine enables it to produce massive peak power of 175 bhp at 9800 rpm and reach from 0-100 km/h in three seconds flat!

Hayabusa was introduced by Suzuki in 1999. It derived its name from the Japanese term for the Peregrine Falcon, the fastest creature on the planet with speed exceeding 300 km/h. Hayabusa was a massive success right from its inception, encouraging other bike manufacturers to come up with similar speedsters. However, none of its competitors was as successful in the US and European markets. The 2008 model carried a MSRP of US$11,999.

LAND TRANSPORT

Kusttram— Belgium's coastal tram

The Belgian Coast Tram is reckoned to be the longest tram line in the world, following almost the entire Belgian coastline from De Panne, on the French border, to Knokke, on the Dutch border. There are a total of 70 stops over 68 km and all the coastal towns and villages can be visited.

It starts right near the border between France and Belgium in the city De Panne and stops in the city Knokke-Heist at the border between Belgium and Netherlands. It crosses sixteen major cities and has seventy stops. A big part of this tramline curves along the North Sea, which definitely offers wonderful landscapes.

The first part of this line was built early in 1885, while the rest was finished after the First World War, with small adjustments in the last decade. The tram comes every twenty minutes in offseason and every ten in the summer. Thousands of Belgians use it every day to commute.

The trams are new, silent and they get you from one end to the other in approximately two hours and twenty minutes. They run from 6:00 am until almost midnight and stops at every station, although you should be careful to push the button and let the driver know you want to get out.

Test Your MEMORY

1. What is land transport?

2. Write briefly the history of land transport.

3. Describe briefly the categories of land transportation.

4. Name the types of land transport vehicles.

5. Describe roads and highways.

6. Write briefly about traffic control.

7. Write the advantages of land transport.

8. Write the disadvantages of land transport.

9. Write about land transport's impact on environment.

10. Write briefly about two famous cars.

11. Write briefly about two famous trains.

12. Write briefly about two famous bikes.

LAND TRANSPORT

Index

A

automobiles 4, 7, 8, 9, 12, 15, 21

B

bicycle 5, 8, 11
Blue Train 27
Bugatti Veyron 21
bus 4, 7, 8, 9

C

camel caravan 4
car 3, 6, 7, 8, 9, 12, 13, 21, 22, 27
Conestoga wagon 4, 8

E

environment 3, 18, 29
Eurostar 25

F

four-wheeled carriages 4

H

highways 12

K

Kusttram 30

L

land transport 3, 4, 8, 10, 17, 18, 20
lectica 6

M

motorcycle 8, 11, 28

O

omnibuses 4, 8, 9

P

plaustrum 6
prairie schooner 4, 8

R

raeda 6
rickshaws 7
roads 3, 4, 5, 7, 10, 12, 13, 18, 20, 23
Rolls-Royce Phantom 22

S

Shinkansen (Bullet trains) 26
stagecoaches 4, 8
Suzuki Hayabusa 29

T

Tata trucks 23
taxi 8, 9
traffic lights 15
train 8, 10, 25, 26, 27
tram 8, 10, 13, 30
Trans Siberian Express 24
two-wheeled carts 4, 6, 8

V

velotaxis 7
Volvo trucks 23

W

wagons 4, 5, 6